W9-BWW-283

Activities for the Family Caregiver

CAREGIVING 101

Scott Silknitter, Suzanne John, RN
Dawn Worsley, ADC/MC/EDU, CDP

Disclaimer

This book is for informational purposes only and is not intended as medical advice, diagnosis, or treatment. Always seek advice from a qualified physician about medical concerns, and do not disregard medical advice because of something you may read within this book. This book does not replace the need for diagnostic evaluation, ongoing physician care, and professional assessment of treatments. Every effort has been made to make this book as complete and helpful as possible. It is important, however, for this book to be used as a resource and idea-generating guide and not as an ultimate source for plan of care.

ISBN 978-1-943285-22-8

Copyright © 2016 by R.O.S. Therapy Systems, L.L.C.
All rights reserved including the right of reproduction in whole or in part.

Published by
R.O.S. Therapy Systems, L.L.C.
Greensboro, NC
888-352-9788
www.ROSTherapySystems.com

Introduction

Activities for the Family Caregiver: Caregiving 101

You are a caregiver. Your loved one needs help. You did not choose to be in this position, and your loved one did not choose to need help, but it has happened. Whether it is short term or long term, the assistance that you will provide is invaluable.

You are playing many roles—Nurse, Cook, Cheerleader, Protector, Advocate, Maid, Cab Driver, and whatever else it takes.

Caregiving is hard because it is hard. Our goal is to help you with practical tips and coaching to ease some of the burden and stress you experience daily.

Depending on your loved one's issue—Dementia, TBI, Stroke, Parkinson's, MS, ALS, Alzheimer's, Lewy Body Dementia, Cancer, Hip

Replacement, Heart Disease, Diabetes, Visual Impairment or some combination, things can and will be challenging.

All of those issues have their own specific symptoms, and they affect your loved one in a unique way. As certain issues progress, your loved one and their abilities may change month to month, day to day, or even hour to hour. As the caregiver you see and deal with it all, whether you are ready to or not.

Our mission is to provide you a foundation to help you engage and care for your loved one. The common sense suggestions and tools in this book are based on decades of proven techniques. These tools can help you engage your loved one in both leisure activities and activities of daily living and improve everyone's quality of life.

Table of Contents

Family Members and Caregivers that have read this book:

____

____

____

____

____

____

____

____

____

____

____

____

____

____

Chapter 1

Leisure Activities, Activities of Daily Living, and Their Benefits

"Activities" can be anything and everything—having a conversation, eating a meal, playing cards, singing a song, getting dressed, or just getting into the car for a drive. For some people, these activities can be easier said than done. Leisure Activities and Activities of Daily Living (ADLs) can be challenging, but we need to figure the ways that work best for you and your loved one using a solid foundation of planning and communication so you both can enjoy the benefits of the activities.

Activities can enhance your loved one's sense of well-being, and promote or enhance their physical, cognitive, and emotional health.

This book was written for you, a caregiver helping a loved one or a friend who may be

suffering from any number of issues. Recognizing the growth in the numbers of those aging in place due to financial need or desire to just be at home, the R.O.S. Engagement Program covered in this book is based on the principles and approaches used by professionals in a skilled setting. This was done for two reasons.

1. Provide family caregivers the knowledge and tools to allow them to engage their loved one.

2. Offer a starting point that will provide continuity of approach regarding care, communication, and information-gathering to minimize changes and acclimation time if your loved one does have to move from home to an institutional setting.

If you choose to use the services of a home care agency while caring for your loved one at home, please ask if they have a Home Care

Certified professional on staff, and make sure that the caregiver you choose has received basic training on Activities and how to engage your loved one. This will assist with continuity of approach, communication, and planning that will benefit both you and your loved one.

Our goal is to help you deliver meaningful programs of interest to your loved one that focus on physical, social, spiritual, cognitive, and recreational activities. Everyone involved in caring for your loved one should be "on the same page" to minimize changes and challenges that your loved one will face.

Therapeutic programs can also promote self-reliance and provide opportunities for creativity, self-expression, self-satisfaction, fun, and self-fulfillment. Some programs can specifically address managing stress, strengthening interpersonal skills, opportunities to learn new skills, or enhance skills your loved one already possesses.

The Benefits of Activities with a Standard Approach

The benefits of being active and engaged in activities are far-reaching for both you and your loved one. An Activities plan should be developed based on your loved one's personal preferences and abilities. Benefits include:

Mental Benefits

Use is or lose it. Keeping your loved one's mind active is critical to helping them maintain their abilities and remain as sharp as possible.

Social Benefits

Activities offer the opportunity for increased social interaction between family members, friends, caregivers, and the one being cared for. Activities create positive experiences and memories for everyone.

Sleep Benefits

As part of a daily routine, activities can improve sleeping at night. If a loved one is

inactive all day, it is likely they will nap periodically. Napping can interrupt good sleep patterns at night.

Self-Esteem Benefits

Activities offered at the right skill level provide your loved one with an opportunity for success. Success during activities improves how your loved one feels about themselves.

Anti-Depression and Anti-Anxiety Benefits

Engaging in activities can reduce symptoms of depression and anxiety. Research has shown a reduction in depression and anxiety through the provision of person-appropriate activities.

Behavioral Benefits

Activities can reduce challenging behaviors when the activity conducted is interesting to your loved one. Offer activities at a skill level that allow your loved one to enjoy the activity.

Caregiver Benefits

Activities result in less stress for the caregiver. When your loved one is participating in

activities, there will be less of a need to respond to behavioral issues. This will allow more opportunities to engage positively with one another.

Activities that your loved one used to enjoy may still be accomplished; they just may be done a little differently.

Patience is vital. Adjustments must be made in preparation and execution to accommodate your loved one's remaining strengths and abilities.

The Four Pillars of Activities

The R.O.S. Engagement Program focuses on the Four Pillars of Activities. These are areas that all caregivers for your loved one should be familiar with to provide continuity of care and give your loved one the greatest opportunity for success to engage and improve the quality of life for everyone.

First Pillar of Activities:
Know your Loved One—Information Gathering and Assessment

Have a Personal History Form completed. Know them—who they are, who they were, and what their functional abilities are today. Make sure all caregivers know this as well.

Second Pillar of Activities:
Communicating and Motivating for Success

Communication is key. Each caregiver must know how to effectively communicate with your loved one and be consistent with techniques.

Third Pillar of Activities:
Customary Routines and Preferences

As best as possible, maintain a routine and daily plan based on your loved one's needs and preferences.

Fourth Pillar of Activities: Planning and Executing Activities

Based on all of the information you have gathered about your loved one, you have the opportunity to offer engaging activities that are appropriate and meet your loved one's personal preferences.

Chapter 2

You, the Family, and Friends

Everyone that comes in contact with your loved one must be on the same page for approach, techniques, and assistance they may offer. As the primary caregiver, you are the one who is with your loved one the most. You are the one who must deal with any issues that arise if someone visiting or helping does not follow the normal routines. Consistency and your ability to communicate what should and should not be done are very important. Stick up for yourself and your loved one.

Put YOUR Mask on First

There will be many challenges to you personally in this caregiving journey that can and will wear you down. As a caregiver, first and foremost, you must take care of yourself in order to be able to assist your loved one. That might be easier said than done, but

please make every effort to do so. The following are some general tips for you.

About You

- Put yourself first (this is not being selfish) —if you are not in good physical or mental health you cannot help anyone.
- It is okay to feel grief, anger, and guilt depending on the day and the situation of the moment. *Everyone does.*
- Arrange some time for yourself.
- Keep a strong support system.
- Do not be afraid to ask for help.
- Keep contact with friends.
- Define priorities; do not try to be all things to all people

Stress

- Recognize your own stress and take steps to minimize. Stress can be exhibited in multiple ways:
  - Anger
  - Helplessness

- Embarrassment
- Grief
- Depression
- Isolation
- Physical illness

Burnout

Burnout for caregivers results from physical and emotional exhaustion.

It is important to realize a family member, spouse, or hired caregiver experiences the same emotions as staff in health care facilities, but may not have the needed support system. Suggestions to avoid burnout:

- Know what makes you angry or impatient. Make a list.
- Look for the reason behind behavior.
- Use relaxation techniques, e.g., deep breathing, imagery, and music.
- Ask for help, and accept help when it is offered!

Caregiving is a challenging road with constant twists and turns, from the change in your role/relationship with your loved one, to dealing with the strains of a 24/7 job of caregiving. As much as you may feel like you are alone, please know that you are not. Millions of family caregivers are dealing with the same issues that you are. Do not be embarrassed to share details about what you are experiencing, and do not be afraid to ask for help. There are individuals, organizations, and support groups throughout the country that are available to you.

There is also a caregiver support book called *Put Your Mask on First,* which is an excellent source of information that addresses the issues of you taking care of you. As this book helps you with the practical side of caregiving for your loved one, *Put Your Mask on First* helps you, the caregiver.

Family and Friends

Not all family members or friends may understand or accept your loved one's situation. They may not understand that your loved one can look the same, but they are no longer the person that everyone knew. This can create conflict. Stay strong. You are the primary caregiver. If it helps to avoid a conflict or stress, please have the others read this book prior to a visit so they can begin to understand the monumental task that you face as a caregiver. Use visits and interactions as teaching moments and to let the visitors know how much their visits mean to you and your loved one.

It can take a while to learn new roles and responsibilities. It is critical, however, to have as many family members and friends involved in your loved one's life as possible. Not just to show your loved one they are cared for, but also to give you, the primary family caregiver, the occasional and much-needed break.

The importance of understanding your family dynamics and the importance of each role an individual plays in the family will lead to better understanding and comprehension for the future.

Whether it is an occasional or weekly visit, each family member can play an important role in your loved one's life. Family members can help with caregiving, giving you a break, or prepare the home to ensure safety and quality of life.

Chapter 3

First Pillar of Activities: Know Your Loved One—Information Gathering and Assessment

Knowing your loved one's individual needs, interests, functional abilities, and capacities will assist you in knowing how to plan and engage in meaningful and quality leisure activities. This is the First Pillar of Activities and will help in designing activities that your loved one can enjoy.

As the primary caregiver, you may already know most of the answers, but this is a good and necessary exercise for you, other family members, and other caregivers to execute. The following are items about your loved one that you are most likely able to provide yourself:

Basic Information

Name, preferred name to be called, age, and date of birth

Background Information

Place of birth, cultural/ethnic background, marital status, children (how many, and their names), religion/church, military service/employment, education level, and primary language spoken

Medical and Dietary/Nutritional Information

Any formal diagnosis, allergies, and food regimen/diets

Habits

Drinking/alcohol, smoking, exercise, and other things that are a daily habit

Physical Status

Abilities/limitations, visual aids, hearing deficits, speech, communication, hand dominance, and mobility/gait

Mental Status

Alertness; cognitive abilities/limitations; orientation to family, time, place, person, routine; ability to follow directions; preference for written or verbal instructions; ability to comprehend and follow one-step versus multi-step directions; safety awareness; safety concerns; etc.

Social Status

One-on-one interaction; being visited; communication with others through written words, phone calls, or other means, such as email or online social networking services

Emotional Status

Level of contentment, outgoing/withdrawn, extroverted/introverted, dependent/independent, easily frustrated, easygoing

Leisure Status

Past, present, and possible future interests; solitary versus social activities; physical versus passive activities

Vision Status

Any impairment they may have

Informal Assessments

Informal assessments are done through interviews, observation, and information gathered through other means. These will allow you and others to "fill in the blanks" of the Personal History Form.

Interviews

Interviews are conducted with your loved one or with family members, friends, or significant others. This can be a simple conversation or an in-depth discussion. However it is done, please make sure to write or record all of the information for future use.

Observations

An observation is what you and others have seen or heard concerning your loved one, e.g., how they interact with others, their behavior, and their responses to questions or statements made by others. This includes body language and expressions. You have probably seen these interactions a thousand times and made a mental note whenever something stuck out. Now, you must write them down for your future use and for others.

Information Gathered Through Other Means

Make a request of family members or friends to help complete a Personal History Form for your loved one. An example of this form is at the back of this book. You also may download a copy of the R.O.S. Personal History Form at www.StartSomeJoy.org.

The interview process is particularly important if your loved one is at risk of becoming socially isolated. Your loved one may become easily

embarrassed by their lack of motor control, which causes them to drop things, or they may grow tired of trying to explain things verbally when nonverbal expression is hindered by facial rigidity. Help your loved one and others break through these barriers by gathering as much information as possible and sharing it with all caregivers—family, informal, and formal.

Your ability to identify past preferences is vital to the planning and execution of an activity, which we will cover in this book. Details matter. Let's look at someone who enjoys gardening.

During their assessments, four people might all say they like "gardening," yet they might not actually have the same activity in mind or enjoy the same activity.

- Person 1—Enjoys going outside, cutting the grass, trimming the hedges, and

weed whacking. Anything less would not meet his preference.

- Person 2—Enjoys getting in the flower beds, planting flowers and vegetables, and tending to her garden on her hands and knees each day for an hour.

- Person 3—Enjoys indoor plants. Enjoys propagating plants, and watering and caring for plants daily.

- Person 4—Enjoys arranging flowers in vases for tables.

As you can see from these examples, details matter. Gather as much information as you can for yourself and all family members and caregivers who may help with your loved one.

The Personal History Form at the back of this book is a starting point to gather as much information as possible.

Functional Levels

In addition to the Personal History Form, you also need to look at your loved one's functional level. When planning meaningful activities based on individual interests, you need to set them up for success based on what they are able to accomplish. For the purposes of this topic, we will address the following four functioning levels:

Level 1

Your loved one has good social skills. They are able to communicate. They are alert and oriented to person, place, and time, and they have a long attention span.

Level 2

Your loved one's social skills are somewhat diminished, and their verbal skills may be impaired as well. Your loved one may have some behavioral symptoms. They may

need something to do, and may have an increased energy level, but they have a shorter attention span.

Level 3

Your loved one's social skills are diminished, and their verbal skills are even more impaired than they were at Level 2. They are also easily distracted. Your loved one may have some visual/spatial perception and balance concerns, and they need maximum assistance with their care.

Level 4

Your loved one has a low energy level, nonverbal communication skills, and they rarely initiate contact with others, however, they may respond if given time and cues.

Chapter 4

Second Pillar of Activities:

Communicating and Motivating for Success

Communicating and motivating for success is the Second Pillar for engaging in an activity with your loved one. The key to effective communication is the ability to listen attentively. This requires all caregivers to use communication techniques that provide an open, nonthreatening environment for your loved one. Listening behavior can either enhance and encourage communication or shut down communication altogether. You need to assess your listening style and be able to assess the listening styles of the other caregivers and family members working with your loved one.

Verbal Communication

Communication is an interactive process where information is exchanged. The ability to respond appropriately, to give feedback on something that was communicated, is just as important as having good listening skills.

Verbal Approaches for Good Communication

- Use exact, short, positive phrases. Repeat twice if necessary.
- Speak slowly.
- Only use words your loved one knows.
- Allow time for your loved one to answer.
- Give one instruction at a time. Provide only the number of steps your loved one can handle at a time.
- Use a warm, gentle tone of voice.
- There is no need to shout, unless your loved one also has a hearing impairment.
- If your loved one is unable to see you because of a visual impairment, be sure

to use verbal cues to let them know you are engaged.

- Talk to your loved one like an adult.

<u>**Verbal Communication Tips**</u>

- Make your presence known when entering a room by saying hello.
- Identify yourself. Do not assume the person knows or remembers who you are.
- If there are others present, address your loved one by name so there is no confusion as to whom you are speaking.
- Indicate the end of a conversation with a loved one who is visually impaired to avoid the embarrassment of leaving your loved one speaking when no one is actually there.
- Speak directly to your loved one.
- Always answer questions, and be specific or descriptive in your responses.
- When giving directions, make the directions as clear as possible. Use "left"

and "right" according to the way your loved one is facing.

- Provide a written summary of information/instructions as needed if memory is an issue.
- When speaking with other caregivers or family members about your loved one while your loved one is present, include your loved one in the conversation if possible. Make sure the conversation is respectful of your loved one. They may move or speak slowly, but assume that they hear everything.
- Avoid battle or direct confrontations. For example, avoid situations wherein you are telling someone to do something.

Nonverbal Communication

Although it may seem that most communication happens verbally, research has shown that actually most communication occurs nonverbally. Nonverbal communication occurs through an individual's body language.

* **Note**: Do not assume that nonverbal communication does not matter to someone who has visual impairment due to macular degeneration, stroke, or some other factor just because you "think" it does not. Nonverbal can also be felt. It is multichannel.

There are five key, nonverbal elements to consider:

Facial Expressions

Be aware of what your facial expressions are conveying to your loved one. Your mood will be mirrored.

Eye Contact

Ensure that you have made eye contact with your loved one and that their attention is focused on you and what you are saying.

Gestures and Touch

Calmly use nonverbal signs, such as pointing, waving, and other hand gestures in combination with your words.

Tone of Voice

The inflection in your voice helps your loved one relate to the words you are saying.

Body Language

Be aware of the position of your hands and arms when talking to your loved one.

* **Note**: When communicating with your loved one, be mindful that their body language may not fully tell how they feel or what they are trying to express because of their physical or cognitive issues. Your body language, however, will be read by your loved one.

Nonverbal Communication Tips

- Always approach your loved one from the front before speaking to them.
- Smile and extend your hand as to shake their hand. Use touch where welcomed.
- Do not touch unexpectedly; it might startle your loved one.

- Place yourself at eye level with the loved one with whom you are speaking.
- Use nonverbal gestures along with words.
- Give nonverbal praises, such as smiles and head nods.
- Be an active listener. Give your loved one opportunities and time to speak.
- Make sure that all caregivers give your loved one the opportunity and time to speak.

Approaches to Successful Communication & Activities

Be Calm

Always approach your loved one in a relaxed and calm demeanor. Remember, your mood will be mirrored by your loved one. Smiles are contagious.

Be Flexible

There is no right or wrong way of completing a task. Offer praise and encouragement for the

effort your loved one puts into a task. If you see your loved one becoming overwhelmed or frustrated, stop the task, and re-approach at another time.

Be Nonresistive

Don't force tasks on your loved one. Adults do not want to be told, "No!" or told what to do. The power of suggestion goes a long way, and you get more with an ounce of sugar than you do a pound of vinegar.

Be Guiding, but Not Controlling

Always use a soft, gentle approach, and remember your tone of voice. Your facial expressions must match the words you are saying.

Barriers to Good Communication

Caregiver barriers and environmental barriers can negatively affect communication with your loved one. Here are some tips on how to eliminate these two barriers.

Caregiver Barriers to Communication

- Slow down when speaking too quickly. Also, speak clearly.
- Use a calm tone of voice, and be aware of your hand movements.
- Never be demanding or commanding.
- Never argue with a person with impaired cognition. You will never win the argument.
- Enter their world. Live their truth.
- Do not offer long explanations when answering questions.
- Do not let your anger and frustration at various situations build and turn into hurtful words.

Environmental Barriers to Communication

- Minimize noise from air conditioners and home appliances.
- Turn off the TV if it is on in the same room where you are trying to talk.
- Be aware of outside traffic noise.

- Replace hearing aid batteries that are whistling.
- Adjust the lighting in the room. If the lighting in a room negatively affects your loved one's vision, they may be more focused on trying to see rather than on communicating with you.

Chapter 5

Third Pillar of Activities: Customary Routines and Preferences

Customary routines and preferences is the Third Pillar in an activities program. Activities can occur all day every day. The question should not be, "When should I do activities?" It is not important to focus on when to do activities. The focus should be on making each and every interaction memorable and always respecting your loved one as an individual.

For the purpose of developing a daily plan of care, we will be discussing two areas: Daily Customary Routine and Activity Preferences. The goal is to gain from your loved one's perspective how important certain aspects of care/activity are to them as an individual.

Daily Customary Routine

Your loved one has distinct lifestyle preferences and routines. These should be preserved to the greatest extent possible. All reasonable accommodation should be made to maintain their lifestyle preferences.

Not accommodating your loved one's lifestyle preferences and routine can contribute to depressed mood or increased behavior symptoms or potentially dangerous situations. When a person feels like their control has been removed and that their preferences are not respected as an individual, it can be demoralizing.

Let's use a simple morning cup of coffee and reading the newspaper as an example.

For years, your loved one woke up every Sunday morning, made a cup of coffee, and sat down to read the newspaper. They took

their coffee with two teaspoons of sugar and sat at the head of the kitchen table to read the paper.

If the impairment has progressed to the point that they cannot enjoy their Sunday morning coffee routine on their own, consider ways you or other caregivers can help them maintain that routine. The little things matter.

Activity Preferences

Activities are a way for individuals to establish meaning in their lives. The need for enjoyable activities does not change based on health needs or age. The only thing that changes is the level of assistance an individual may need in order to engage in those pursuits.

A lack of opportunity to engage in meaningful and enjoyable activities can result in boredom, depression, and behavioral disturbances.

Individuals vary in the activities they prefer, reflecting unique personalities, past interest,

perceived environmental constraints, religious and cultural background, and changing physical and mental abilities. We as family caregivers have a great opportunity to empower a loved one to see that they possess many great talents and abilities. By modifying or adapting an activity to allow them to engage at an independent level, you are restoring their self-esteem and self-worth.

Chapter 6

Fourth Pillar of Activities: Planning and Executing Activities

Planning and executing activities is the Fourth Pillar in engaging a loved one in an activity. In order to do that, activities can be spontaneous, but generally must be planned and appropriate for your loved one in order to offer the greatest opportunity for success. Please note that schedules, routines, and plans should be followed. However, they may need to be adapted due to specific issues your loved one may be experiencing that day.

As you plan your loved one's activities as part of the customary routine, you need to consider how an activity fits within the following criteria:

- Person Appropriate—Desires and Preferences
- Person Appropriate—Abilities and Functional Levels

Person Appropriate— Desires and Preferences

Person appropriate refers to the idea that each person has a personal identity and history. It also means that the caregiver has to make sure that all caregivers understand the concept of a specific activity because the name of the activity can mean different things to different people.

Remember our gardening example:

- Person 1—Enjoys going outside, cutting the grass, trimming the hedges, and weed whacking. Anything less would not meet his preference.
- Person 2—Enjoys getting in the flower beds, planting flowers and vegetables, and tending to her garden on her hands and knees each day for an hour.
- Person 3—Enjoys indoor plants. Enjoys propagating plants, and watering and caring for plants daily.

- Person 4—Enjoys arranging flowers in vases for tables.

Remember, when planning activities, you need to ensure that the activity is person appropriate, based on the specific desires and preferences of your loved one.

Person Appropriate—Abilities and Functional Levels

This concept is also based on the idea that each person has a personal identity and history, but it also takes into account the varying functional levels at which a person may be able to participate in an activity. The effects of age, declining health, and other diseases on a person's physical and mental abilities, at some point may mean that while many activities can still be performed, some activities may be facilitated through certain modifications, e.g., by using adaptive equipment.

Based on your loved one's functional level and abilities, some activities may also be done as a group activity. This creates an opportunity for socialization, interaction, and conversation between you and your loved one.

The Lesson Plan

In order to keep all caregivers up-to-date and informed as to your loved one's ability to participate in an activity, we suggest using an activity Lesson Plan to document everything.

The Lesson Plan template at the end of this chapter is a guideline for an activity. It is an ever-changing document. It is meant to be written on to note the changes you made in the original plan so the family member or caregiver working with your loved one next can follow your modifications in the hopes of recreating a positive experience.

Items in the Lesson Plan

Date

Document the date the activity is used with your loved one.

Activity Name

Give the activity a name that you or your loved one prefers.

Objective of Activity

Our goal is to provide meaningful activities. People have a need to be productive, and they want to engage in something with a purpose. List the objectives of the activity.

Materials

List suggested materials to be used with this activity.

Prerequisite Skills

These are the skills your loved one needs in order to participate in this activity.

Activity Outline

These are step-by-step instructions to complete this activity.

Evaluation

When you or a family member are conducting an activity with your loved one, documenting results and responses is critical to identifying ways to improve activity programs for your loved one. Items to document should include:

- Verbal cues, physical assistance, or modifications you make to this activity.
- How your loved one responded to this activity.
- Whether your loved one enjoyed this activity. What did they like or dislike about the activity?
- Whether the activity was successful at distracting or eliminating a negative behavior. Why and how was it successful?

A blank template is included on the next page to give you an example of what a Lesson Plan looks like.

* **Note:** Make sure caregivers and family members are consistent with the type of verbal cues, physical assistance, or modifications that produce positive results.

Lesson Plan Blank Example

Date	Activity Name
Objective of Activity	
Materials	
Prerequisite Skills	
Room Lighting	
Activity Outline	
Evaluation	

Chapter 7

Leisure Activity Categories, Tips, and Suggestions

Activity Categories

Activities are generally broken down into three different categories: maintenance activities, supportive activities, and empowering activities.

Maintenance Activities

Maintenance activities are traditional activities that help your loved one maintain physical, cognitive, social, spiritual, and emotional health. Examples include:

- Using manipulative games, such as those from R.O.S. Therapy Systems
- Craft and art activities
- Attending church services

- Working trivia and crossword puzzles like the R.O.S. *How Much Do You Know About* puzzle series in Amazon or the R.O.S. Store
- Taking a walk

Supportive Activities

If your loved one has a lower tolerance for traditional activities, supportive activities provide a comfortable environment while providing stimulation or solace. Examples include:

- Listening to and singing music
- Hand massages
- Relaxation activities, such as aromatherapy, meditation, and bird-watching

Empowering Activities

Empowering activities help your loved one attain self-respect by offering

opportunities for self-expression and exercising responsibility. Examples include:

- Cooking
- Making memory boxes
- Folding laundry

General Activity Tips

Travel Tips for Moving from Room to Room or Place to Place

- When escorting your loved one, ask them if they need assistance. If they do not request any assistance, walk side-by-side or a half step behind.

- Please remember your communication techniques—be calm, be flexible, be guiding, but not controlling. There is no need to yell or startle your loved one while they are working through taking a step. If you are in public, yelling may draw unwanted attention to them, causing them to focus on potentially

being embarrassed rather than on taking a step.

- If your loved one does require some assistance, offer your arm for your loved one to hold onto or interlock with. Find the easiest and most comfortable way to walk together. Walk side-by-side or a half pace ahead while providing verbal cues about the environment.
- Announce when you are approaching doorways, stairs, and ramps.
- Avoid puddles, snowbanks, and other natural barriers.
- Avoid cracked tile, untacked throw rugs, and protruding floorboards.

Writing and Coloring Activity Tips

- If your loved one has trouble holding a pen or pencil, wrap foam around the shaft of the pen to help your loved one's grip. You can try cutting a piece from a

foam noodle used in a swimming pool to fit on the writing tool.

- Reduce glare and shadowing by positioning a chair and table so any natural light is behind your loved one instead of coming at them from the front.
- To prevent shadows, place lamps on the opposite side of the hand being used. Locate the bottom edge of the lampshade just below eye level.
- Shiny paper can increase glare, so it is best to use matte paper when reading or writing.
- Use large-print crossword, word search, or word scramble puzzles. If you cannot find the R.O.S. *How Much Do You Know About* puzzle series or other large-print sources, most copiers have the ability to increase the size of the print.
- A dry-erase board or tablet may also be used to practice writing.

* **Note:** Know the type of seating where your loved one is the most comfortable when they are writing, and, if possible, move them to that seat.

* **Note:** If your loved one is seated in a wheelchair, recliner, or bed, provide a flat surface that fits in their lap to place paper on.

Reading Activity Tips

- Large-print books are available at most bookstores and libraries.
- Read to your loved one, or take turns reading to each other.
- Listen to audiotapes and books on CD borrowed from your local library, or from the free Talking Books program sponsored by the National Library Service.
- If your loved one prefers reading to listening, many new mobile devices such

as iPads, Kindles, and Nooks all have options to increase the font size and adjust the color contrast.

- Try the Book Strap from R.O.S. Therapy Systems to help keep a book and the page in place.

Craft Activity Tips

- Make sure that supplies are easily accessible.
- Empower your loved one by choosing an area of the home where they can most comfortably participate.
    - If at a table and in a wheelchair, make sure the wheelchair can fit under the table.
    - If in a recliner, use an activity surface that fits comfortably in their lap, and choose an activity that does not have too many pieces that may be hard to keep track of.

- Craft Boxes and Materials
  - Place craft activity supplies in boxes clearly labeled with a broad-tipped black marker.
  - Group like items for activities together.
  - Store materials in different shaped/sized containers for easier recognition.
  - Choose identifying and organizational systems that work best for your loved one.

Music Tips

Music has health benefits. Listening to music can help with many common disease symptoms, including pain.

People who listen to music for one hour a day for one week—whether they picked the tunes themselves or researchers

provided them—felt more empowered, and reported less pain, depression, and disability than those who did not listen to music. Average pain ratings among people who listened to music fell by about 20 percent, whereas pain among nonlisteners actually increased.

Classical music is one of the best choices. Listening to slow-tempo classical music may ease pain. Music can be very powerful.

If classical music is not your loved one's cup of tea, try jazz or new age genres. Here are a few suggestions of both types:

- Beethoven for Relaxation
- Chopin for Relaxation
- Vivaldi for Relaxation
- Music for Sound and Healing

If you do not have an iPod or radio handy, singing works as well.

Game Playing Activity Tips

Playing Cards:

- If needed, use adaptive equipment to place the playing cards in while your loved one is seated at a table.
- The Card Holder Board Insert from R.O.S. Therapy Systems allows your loved one to have the card holder in their lap while seated in a recliner or wheelchair.

Puzzles:

- Choose puzzles with larger pieces. These are easier for your loved one to manipulate.
- If your loved one becomes frustrated because puzzle pieces are sliding when being placed, try a magnetic puzzle and a metallic flat surface so the pieces stick when placed.

Active Activity Suggestions

In addition to the tips for general activities, please review the following suggestions for active activities. As you build these activities into your loved one's life, please make sure to schedule opportunities for rest after or between activities.

Active activities can be broken into four areas that all can help improve the quality of life for your loved one.

Aerobic Activities

During aerobic activities, the body's large muscles move in a rhythmic manner for a sustained period of time. Aerobic activities help to maintain or improve cardiovascular health.

Strengthening Activities

Strengthening activities improve overall muscle strength, walking speed, posture, and overall physical fitness.

Flexibility Activities

Flexibility or stretching exercises improve mobility, increase range of motion, reduce stiffness, and can help reduce the risk of injury.

Balance Activities

Balance activities improve posture and stability.

* **Note:** Depending on the activity or exercise, you, a family member, or a trained professional should always be there to supervise and assist your loved one as needed.

Aerobic Activities

Objectives of aerobic activities include improving physical fitness and having positive effects on slowness, stiffness, and mood.

Examples of aerobic activities for your loved one:

- Walking
    - with you, a family member, or your dog
    - on a treadmill
    - around the shopping mall
- Swimming or water aerobics
    - at your gym or YMCA
- Dancing
    - at home with you, a family member, or a friend
    - at a local dance hall, club, or ballet center
- Chair aerobics
    - in your living room following along with a video
    - at your local gym or YMCA

Strengthening Activities

The objective of improving muscle strength is to facilitate everyday activities, such as getting up from a chair, moving from room to room in the home, and making any task easier to manage.

Examples of strengthening activities for your loved one:

- Weights/resistance
  - free weight activities/exercises
  - elastic bands activities/exercises
  - body weight activities/exercises
- Yard work or gardening

What strengthening activities will your loved one enjoy, and where will they be done?

Flexibility Activities

Objectives of stretching and flexibility activities include improving range of motion, which can affect posture and walking ability, reducing the risk of injury, and making every-day activities easier.

Examples of flexibility activities for your loved one:

- Gentle stretching
  - In your living room following along with a video

- Yoga, including chair yoga
- Bilateral arm training with rhythmic auditory cueing (BATRAC)
- Treadmill-supported walking
- Strengthening or resistance training

Balance Activities

Balance activities can improve posture and stability. Preserving your loved one's ability to maintain their balance can help to reduce the likelihood of falling, potentially calm your loved one's fears of falling, and help them generally in performing daily tasks.

Examples of balance activities for your loved one:

- Yoga, including chair yoga
- At-home balance exercises using
    - A Wii
    - A balance ball or balance pillow

What balance activities will your loved one enjoy, and where will they be done?

Chapter 8

Activities of Daily Living Tips and Suggestions

Unlike the leisure activities discussed, the activities of daily living covered in this book are a necessary part of everyday life. The following pages contain tips and suggestions for you to use with your loved one. These tips are particularly helpful for those functioning at a level that requires moderate to total assistance.

Energy Conservation and Rest

The body requires tremendous energy to heal or perform when not at a 100 percent functioning capacity. Energy conservation and rest are important in relation to your loved one's unique situation. You, as the caregiver, need to evaluate and determine your loved one's level of functioning and where/when energy conservation needs to be

implemented. As the day is scheduled, make sure to plan periods of rest between necessary daily activities.

The simplification of daily tasks will conserve energy for your loved one. If your loved one uses less energy on one task, it can help them have more energy for other activities throughout the day. Your loved one will expend different levels of energy with different activities (bathing, dressing, toileting, etc.). Evaluate your loved one's performance of an activity and decide if it is performed as efficiently as possible. Never underestimate the energy needed for activities requiring a lot of thought (cognition)—in addition to the obvious physical effort required for an activity. Even when your loved one is experiencing physical and/or cognitive impairments, you always want to encourage them to be as independent as safely possible.

All activities of the day should be planned out to the greatest extent possible—this includes

personal care routines, leisure activities, chores, and exercise. They should be spaced throughout the day, with the items that require the most energy being accomplished at the time of day your loved one feels the best. For some this may be morning; for others afternoon; and evening might be best for a few.

Do not schedule too many things to do in one day, and be prepared to cancel some plans if your loved one is not feeling well or up to it. It is better to do fewer things over a few days than try to do them all in one day and create exhaustion and possible physical discomfort for days because of poor pacing.

Discuss with your loved one, ahead of time, your level of assistance with certain activities on days with higher activities or when an additional activity is being incurred. For example, Grandma usually takes 45 minutes to dress, toilet, and brush her teeth in the morning and has a 30-minute nap two hours

after that activity. Today, you are taking her to a doctor appointment at 1:00 p.m. If you assist with the dressing portion of her morning activity, she can conserve and utilize that energy for the doctor's appointment. While efficient planning is your greatest asset, the ability to adjust and accommodate other circumstances is vital. Remember to openly communicate the day's events and encourage independence in activities as safety permits.

If your loved one becomes tired during an activity, allow for pause and rest. If your loved one turns a rest period into a nap, be careful not to let the nap go too long during the day, as sleep may become elusive at night. Keeping awake/sleep patterns is as important as routine daily activities.

Bathing

Bathing can be a relaxing, enjoyable experience—or a time of confrontation and anger. If your loved one needs assistance with

bathing, use a calm approach. Your loved one's "usual" routine is very important, and maintaining their routine allows for a certain level of control for them during a very personal activity.

Safety

- Water temperature should range from 110–115 degrees Fahrenheit maximum to prevent burning or skin injury. Use your elbow to check the water temperature—hands are not consistent indicators of temperatures.
- Hot water can cause fatigue.
- The floor of the tub needs to be slip resistant. Use a rubber mat that does not slide, or use permanent nonslip decals.
- Place a nonskid rug on the floor outside the tub to prevent slipping.

- Install grab bars. Always make sure the grab bars are properly and securely installed into the wall studs.
- Utilize a bath/shower chair if necessary.
- Do not use bath oils.

Bathing—Know Your Loved One

- Is your loved one accustomed to a bath or shower?
- Does your loved one need assistance to get into the bath or shower?
- Can your loved one soap their body or wash their hair alone?
- Can your loved one independently dry with a towel? A simple trick is to sew straps onto the towel, making the towel easier to hold.
- If help is needed, who is your loved one the most comfortable with when bathing?

- It can be awkward waiting and watching someone perform such a personal task. As the caregiver, you can provide supervision, but be involved in another activity within the space. For instance, getting towels out while your loved one is undressing is an effective use of the time. Washing your loved one's lower body while they wash their upper body can deflect this discomfort. This also creates a sense of support versus a feeling of total dependence.

Bathing—Communicating and Motivating

If you have to help a loved one bathe:

- Allow your loved one to do what is safely within their control.
- Stay friendly and respectful. Be "gently guiding."
- Try to avoid arguments by offering a combination of visual cues, step-by-step setup, and short verbal cues.

- If something of an embarrassing nature occurs, find a way to make light of the incident.

Bathing—Customary Routines and Preferences

- What time of day does your loved one normally bathe?
- How often did your loved one bathe prior to the physical or cognitive impairment?
- What is the process that works for you and your loved one when it is time to bathe? Create a document that details the process so all caregivers know each detail of the process.

  For example, is the water turned on and running prior to your loved one entering the tub? Is a towel placed on a shower chair that your loved one may use so that the chill on his or her bottom is removed when sitting?

- Whatever the process, take it one step at a time, following your loved one's normal bathing routine. For example, your loved one may prefer that you wash their hair first and then their body. If sitting in the tub, they may like to soak for 10 minutes before washing.
- When assisting your loved one, have a towel ready to put over their shoulders or on their lap to minimize feelings of exposure. Maintain privacy—close blinds, curtains, and doors. Avoid drafts.
- Be sure to have your loved one's favorite personal care products for familiar smell and feeling. Making a bath/shower caddy of their favorite products is a good idea.

Bathing—Planning and Executing

- Have all care items and tools ready prior to starting the bath process.
    - A shower chair if necessary

  - A handheld hose for showering and bathing
  - A long-handled sponge or scrubbing brush if self-scrubbing is desired
  - Sponges with soap inside or a soft soap applicator instead of bar soap (bar soap can easily slip out of your loved one's hand)

- Have a towel and clothing prepared for when the bath is finished.
- A second towel can be placed on the back of a chair to allow your loved one to dry his or her back by rubbing on the towel or you might use a terry cloth robe instead of a towel for drying.
- Always use bath time to observe and assess your loved one's skin health. Document any concerns or changes that you might notice, and use this as a communication tool with other caregivers.

Other Bathroom & Grooming Activities

Encourage your loved one to maintain personal grooming habits. Your loved one may need physical/cognitive assistance and/or both. If your loved one has participated in occupational therapy, utilize the adaptive and compensatory strategies and tips from rehabilitation for optimum independence. For example, you may need to set up the space so that bathing items are easy to reach, adjust shower seating, or use a handheld shower, a checklist for the steps of the task, or teamwork for the hardest parts of the task.

It can sometimes be easier to "do things" for your loved one to save time and mess. In the long run, this serves to make your loved one more dependent. Encouraging independence for as long as possible is a key goal and is essential to their overall health.

- Allow plenty of time for routines. If having your loved one do everything independently takes more time than

available, select two to four tasks that are most important. Keep the big picture in mind. Your loved one may value being outdoors, volunteering, or exercising more. If time is a factor, save time in personal care routines, and spend time on the activities that bring your loved one the most satisfaction. This is where the evaluating discussed at the beginning of Chapter 8 comes into play. Communicate and reach agreements on how you can assist. This allows your loved one to feel in "control" and fosters feelings of independence.

- Having someone brush your loved one's teeth is not always a comfortable feeling. Always allow him or her to do what is safely possible. Adaptive grips might help for holding onto the toothbrush. Electric brushes can compensate for fine motor deficits and often include a timer indicating how long to brush.

- Helping your loved one maintain oral hygiene is very important. Poor oral hygiene can lead to additional health problems including gum disease, mouth sores, and infections. Declining nutritional status can occur from prolonged poor oral hygiene.

Encourage your loved one to keep up with personal grooming, such as shaving, makeup application, and hair care. Provide physical assistance as needed. Large grip items may help with fine motor challenges.

- Use an electric razor for safety.
- Give positive feedback, and avoid pointing out small mistakes. Be gently guiding in your approach.
- If your loved one had been accustomed to wearing makeup, there is no reason for this to stop. If your loved one shows interest or a desire to wear makeup, encourage the familiar routine and offer

assistance to apply it if needed. Explore built-up grips for brushes and combs. Consider teaching them to stabilize the elbow on the counter or sink to provide more control of the hand.

Hair

- Try to maintain the hairstyle and hair care routine to which your loved is familiar. However, if independence is more important, consider a style that allows this independence.

Toileting or Using the Bathroom

- Learn your loved one's individual toileting habits and routines. This might not be something you needed knowledge of before their physical/cognitive changes, but it is necessary now to accommodate your changing role in your loved one's care.

- The best approach is to offer the toilet routinely on rising, or upon awakening from a nap. Also, offer the toilet at least 30 to 40 minutes after meals and at bedtime. You will readily learn your loved one's habits, notice when changes occur, and notice when outside factors might influence changes. It is recommended to keep a record or journal to communicate this routine with other caregivers.

- If your loved one suffers with communication difficulties due to their changing physical/cognitive capabilities, watch for nonverbal clues, such as agitation, pulling at the clothes, crying, or restlessness. This may indicate a need to use the bathroom.

- When needed, help with clothing, and be positive and pleasant while assisting.

- Provide verbal cues and instructions as needed. Be guiding, but not controlling.

- If your loved one has fine motor deficits, clothing with minimal fasteners, elastic-waist pants, or stretch pants can be more easily pulled up/down and help make toileting less difficult.

- Be sure to provide other caregivers/ providers information regarding the toileting schedule of your loved one when they are outside the home setting.

- Know the public toilet access prior to going somewhere. Not all public bathrooms are user friendly, despite being "accessible." This will help reduce any possible anxiety your loved one may have in regards to toileting when on an outing.

Clothing

Clothing—Know Your Loved One

- Your loved one may maintain the same style of clothes worn before their physical/cognitive changes began.

- If personal care is a challenge, clothes need to be comfortable and easy to remove, especially for toileting.
- Choose clothes that are loose fitting and have elastic waistbands. Items with larger buttons are easier to manipulate.
- If possible, choose clothing that opens in the front, not the back. This prevents your loved one from having to reach behind the body and encourages independence when dressing.
- When your loved one suffers from physical deficits that involve their motor skills, look for clothing with large, flat buttons, Velcro closures, zippers, or elastic waistbands when purchasing new items of clothing.
- To assist your loved one with zipping pants or a jacket, attach a zipper pull or leather loop on the end of the zipper.

- If bending and tying shoes is problematic, consider slip-on shoes. Non-tie shoes are very popular now. There are also elastic type shoestrings that allow previously tied shoes to become slip-ons.

Clothing—Routines and Preferences

- If your loved one has trouble paying attention and making choices, you may have to limit the clothing choices you offer, and leave only two outfit options in the room at a time.
- If your loved one wants to wear the same thing every day, and if you can afford it, buy three or four sets of the same clothing.

Clothing—Planning and Executing

- Clothes should be laid out according to what goes on first. This should be determined by your loved one's preferred routine.

- Avoid clothes that are most difficult for your loved one, such as panty hose, knee-high nylons, tight socks, or high heels.

- Make sure that items are not inside out and that buttons, zips, and fasteners are all undone before handing the clothes to your loved one.

- Be sure clothing is neat and clean. Appearance influences one's dignity and self-esteem.

Dressing

Dressing—Know Your Loved One

Your loved one may just need verbal cues and instructions on dressing. Please remember to allow independent dressing as much as possible, for as long as safely possible, to foster an ongoing sense of dignity and independence. Be gently guiding. As the primary caregiver, you will need to assess

when your loved one's abilities change, and communicate to all caregivers to assist accordingly.

Dressing—Communicating and Motivating

- When providing instruction to your loved one, use short simple sentences.
- If your loved one suffers from cognitive impairments, give instructions in very short steps, such as, "Now put your arm through the sleeve." It is helpful to use actions to demonstrate these instructions.
- Remember to offer the toilet before getting dressed.
- Avoid "hovering" while your loved one is dressing. You need to be available as needed during the process, but you can do another task, like make the bed or straighten up, so your loved one does not feel so slow or incompetent, or that you are waiting on them.

Dressing—Routines and Preferences

- Does your loved one get dressed first thing in the morning—before breakfast or after breakfast?
- Does your loved one change into pajamas right before bed or after dinner?
- Try to maintain your loved one's preferred routine for as long as possible.
- Little things matter. For example, your loved one may like to put on all of their underwear before putting on anything else. Maintaining this routine encourages their feelings of control in their life.

Dressing—Planning and Executing

- If there are others living in the house, remember to provide privacy. Close blinds or curtains, close the door, and put a do not disturb "dressing" sign out to ensure privacy.

- If your loved one suffers with physical ailments, such as one-sided weakness, dress the weak side first. When removing clothes, it is recommended that you undress the strong side first.

- If mistakes are made—for example, by putting something on the wrong way—be tactful, or find a way for both of you to laugh about it.

* **Note:** Wearing several layers of thin clothing rather than one thick layer can be helpful. With layers, your loved one will be able to remove a layer if too warm. Remember that your loved one may not be able to tell you if he or she gets too hot or cold, so keep an eye out for signs of discomfort.

Eating

Eating—Know Your Loved One

- Keep long-standing personal preferences in mind when preparing food. However, be aware that your loved one may

suddenly develop new food preferences or reject foods that they once enjoyed. Again, a journal or notebook with this information is a good idea for communicating to other caregivers.

- Can your loved one eat independently?
- Does your loved one have a visual impairment that may affect their ability to see a meal or drink? You would want to accommodate the table setting accordingly.
- Due to normal age-related changes in eyesight, eating and dining may offer additional challenges—even if your loved one suffered no visual impairment in relation to any specific health diagnosis.
- A special diet might need to be followed depending on your loved one's health issues. Please follow the directions and guidance provided by the medical professionals with whom you work.

- A soft food diet may need to be followed, or foods might need to be pureed or liquefied. Be sure the home has an appliance capable of performing this task.

Eating—Communicating and Motivating

- Use short, simple sentences.
- Provide verbal cues and instructions as needed.
- Give your loved one your full attention.
- Be guiding, but not controlling.

Eating—Routines and Preferences

- Factor into the overall daily schedule that it may take an hour or longer to finish each meal or snack.
- Keep mealtimes simple, and keep the routine that was familiar prior to the physical or cognitive impairment. Encourage your loved one to eat in an upright position, especially if swallowing difficulties exist.

- If eating out was common, consider each restaurant's accessibility. Try to avoid rush hour, if extra time is needed. Make sure to get seating that fits a wheelchair or that optimizes independence. Some restaurants will puree foods if needed. Call ahead and inquire if your loved one's needs can be met at their facility.

* **Note:** Remember, your loved one's sense of taste may change. Food that was eaten for years may no longer be enjoyable. Make note of any changes in your loved one's food preferences on their Personal History Form.

Eating—Planning and Executing

This simple, everyday activity requires maneuvering objects, as well as other skills that many of us may take for granted. You and your loved one will need to develop techniques that work for your loved one. Again, document what is/isn't successful to communicate with other caregivers.

- It is completely appropriate to ask your loved one if assistance is desired.
- Offer to dish the food onto your loved one's plate if needed.
- Cut foods prior to serving if necessary. When cutting food, make sure the pieces are small enough for your loved one to chew and swallow easily. If necessary, puree or serve "soft" foods.

If your loved one has visual deficits, create clear visual distinctions between the table, the dishes, and the food.

- Use solid colors with no distracting patterns.
- When pouring a light-colored drink, such as milk, use a dark glass.
- When pouring a dark-colored drink, such as cola, use a white glass.
- Avoid clear glasses. They can disappear from view.

- Use white dishes when serving dark-colored food, and use dark dishes when serving light-colored food.
- If a unilateral-sided weakness is present, adjust the table setting accordingly. For example, if your loved one has limited vision in their right eye, you want to avoid placing silverware and drinking glasses on the right side of their plate or table. Put the items within their reach on the side of their strength.
- To make dishes easier to find on the table, use a tablecloth or placemats that are the opposite color of the dishes.

  * **Note:** Fiesta ware colors (yellow/ tangerine) contrast with most foods so they can be easily seen and will enhance visual perception.

- Use adaptive utensils if needed. These can be purchased or created on your own utilizing products around your home.

- Use a long straw with a no-spill cup or use a plastic mug with a large handle if needed.
- Be sure there is proper lighting in the room to reduce glare.

Other Meal Considerations

- If your loved one's ability to discern food temperatures is affected, test the temperature of foods and beverages before serving. There is silverware available that changes color if the food is too hot.
- Make meals an enjoyable social event, so everyone looks forward to the experience.
- Clean up spills immediately.
- If your loved one wants to assist in making a meal, accommodate and allow them to be safely involved. Give tasks that they will be successful at accomplishing.

Meal Preparation Tips

If your loved one wants to help prepare meals and can safely assist or independently perform, here are some tips to make meal preparation a little easier:

- Labeling cabinets can improve independence by making it easier to locate items.
- Use simple, step-by-step written or verbal instructions.
- Consider writing out steps and checking off tasks as completed.
- Use proper equipment and modifications for cutting food. There is a variety of adaptive cooking tools available, from specialized cutting boards for one-handed individuals, built-up utensils, electric can openers, and timers for memory problems, to mats for stabilizing equipment.

- Provide supervision and/or assistance as needed to ensure your loved one's safety.
- When utilizing a stove top, use the back burners, and turn the handles inward toward the back of the stove. This technique can help avoid potential grabbing of the pots or pans, thus minimalizing a burn risk.
- If you are not there to supervise a meal due to work or other obligation, consider structuring and setting up the parts of the task so that your loved one can safely and independently complete them with success.
- If your loved one is able to manage basic food preparation, yet stove top cooking and/or cutting is problematic, consider putting individual meals in a microwaveable container with a label for cook time—or plan cold meals, such as sandwiches.

Chapter 9

Home Preparation

You and your loved one need to feel comfortable, capable, and safe in your home. As the Four Pillars of Engagement are the foundation for all activities, preparation of your home is crucial.

General Organization and Environment

When organizing your loved one's environment, be sure to do it ***with*** them, not for them. Label drawers and cabinets, and make sure there is easy access to a phone. The following are general tips that caregivers and family members can use to prepare the home to accommodate your loved one's needs. Decide what works for you and your loved one.

Home Safety Checklist: Bedroom		
Issue	Y/N	Options
Lighting Is lighting adequate?		Add light-sensored night-light. Place touch lamp on nightstand. Place rope lighting along hallway leading to bathroom.
Room Clutter Is there too much furniture, too many extra pillows, or too many "stacks of stuff"?		Remove ALL extra furnishings and unnecessary "stacks of stuff." Leave favorite items.
Furniture Clutter Are dresser and nightstand cluttered?		Remove ALL items from nightstand that are not functional and needed. Leave the following items: lamp, phone, plastic drinking glass with top and straw, place for reading glasses and hearing aids. Remove ALL unnecessary items from top of dresser to avoid confusion. Remove unnecessary items and box for storage, donation, or disposal.

Home Safety Checklist: Bedroom		
Issue	**Y/N**	**Options**
Tripping Hazards		
Are there tripping hazards?		Remove all throw and scatter rugs. Fix or replace loose floorboards.
Are there rugs or carpets that can be tripped on?		Have professionals restretch loose carpeting to remove lumps and ridges if needed.
Are cords from lamps, TV, or radio out of the way?		Move cords out of walking area. Bundle cords together and attach to baseboards or behind furniture.
Are pathways clear?		Remove any loose items from floor or pathway from room. Organize and box for proper storage, donation, or disposal.
Is there enough room for walking aids?		Make pathway wide enough to accommodate people, wheelchairs, and walking aids.
Furniture		
Is furniture sturdy enough to provide support if needed?		Antique bedside tables should be replaced with sturdy nightstands. If possible, there should be a chair with sturdy arms and legs that is the same height as the bed.
Is bed a sensible height to get into and out of?		Sensible height is if person's thighs are parallel to the floor and feet are flat on the floor when seated on edge of the bed. Change out decorative bed frame for a practical bed frame if necessary.

Home Safety Checklist: Bedroom		
Issue	**Y/N**	**Options**
Bedding		
Is it sensible and practical? Is it too heavy to be moved easily?		Without removing your loved one's favorite blanket, lighten covers as much as possible.
Is there an electric blanket or heating pad?		Never use electric blankets or electric mattress pads. Only use heating pads in chairs and never use for extended sleeping hours.

Home Safety Checklist: Closets		
Issue	**Y/N**	**Options**
Lighting		
Is lighting adequate?		Install task lighting if needed.
Is light pull chain easily accessible?		If possible, change pull chain light fixture to light fixture with switch.
Shelving		
Are shelves easy to reach?		Shelving should be located at a height that person using it can reach items without stretching.
Are shelves original from builder?		Consider removing original shelving from builder and replacing with new, easier-access shelves.
Shoes		
Can shoes be reached without bending over?		If bending is an issue, consider installing an over-the-door shoe rack.
Clothing		
Is closet full of clothing that is no longer being worn?		Never remove your loved one's favorite outfit. Remove unworn or worn out clothing. Leave choices that are easy to match. Keep clothes that are easy to put on and take off.
Are shelves stuffed with a hodgepodge of items that may tumble and fall?		Resolve shelving issue by removing unneeded items and organizing items to box and store, donate, or dispose of.

Home Safety Checklist: Bathroom		
Issue	**Y/N**	**Options**
Lighting		
Is lighting adequate?		Install task lighting if needed.
Is light switch easily accessible?		Change pull chain light to light with switch if possible.
Color Contrast		
Is the bathroom all white or light colors?		Change wall color so it contrasts with fixtures and counters.
Toilet		
Is toilet at a height that allows your loved one to sit and stand comfortably?		If possible, add a seat riser or a 3-in-1 commode over the toilet. If possible, replace toilet with a taller model. If possible, install grab bars on both sides at an angle that best suits person who needs them the most.
Mirror		
Is mirror positioned for sitting and standing?		Mirrors may need to be covered or removed for those with dementia as the person may no longer recognize themselves.
Does mirror cause fear or confusion?		Mirrors can be removed or covered with a window shade that can be raised or lowered.
Floor Mats and Rugs		
Is the bathroom floor all white or light colors?		Use rug that is secured with double-sided tape or non-skid padding. Don't use a dark rug—a person with dementia may mistake a dark rug for a hole in the floor.

Home Safety Checklist: Bathroom		
Issue	**Y/N**	**Options**
Additional Seating Is the bathroom large enough for a chair?		Use a chair in the bathroom to help your loved one while drying themselves after bath or to rest as needed.
Temperature Is the bathroom warm enough?		Some people may get cold easily and need the bathroom warmer than others. A portable heater could be used to warm the bathroom prior to use, but heater should be removed before using the bathroom.
Tub/Shower Does tub/shower have decorative glass doors?		Remove glass doors and replace with a shower curtain.
Are faucets clearly marked *Hot* and *Cold*?		Replace or remark *Hot* and *Cold* faucets.
Are shampoos, conditioners, and soaps in pump dispensers?		Pump dispensers are easier to use than bottles that must be squeezed and/or turned upside down to dispense.
Is there a shower chair available?		Showers can be exhausting. Using a shower chair to rest can help prevent someone from becoming too weak and falling during the shower.
Grab Bars Are there grab bars to make getting into and out of tub or shower easier?		Grab bars should be installed properly and securely into wall studs–not just into tile or fiberglass. Avoid use of suction cups as they can be unreliable.

Home Safety Checklist: Halls and Stairs		
Issue	Y/N	Options
Lighting Is lighting adequate?		Use a plug-in night-light. Install light switches on both ends of hallway.
Obstacles Are there obstacles or clutter in hallway?		Remove ALL clutter. Organize and box for proper storage, donation, or disposal—no matter what the item is.
Are there loose floorboards or rugs in hallway?		Repair all loose floorboards. Remove all throw rugs.
Is there furniture in hallway?		Remove all furniture.
Are there doors in hallway?		Keep all doors closed at all times.
Smoke/Carbon Monoxide Detectors Are carbon monoxide and smoke detectors installed?		Install working units on all levels. Replace batteries semiannually.
Handrails Are there handrails in hallway and stairwell?		Install handrails on both sides of hallway and stairwell or secure existing rails.
Stairs Are steps easily seen?		Use neon striping, paint, or duct tape to mark edges of stairs.
Walkers Are walkers easily accessible and transportable?		If possible, keep separate walkers at top and bottom of stairs.

Home Safety Checklist: Kitchen		
Issue	**Y/N**	**Options**
Lighting Is lighting bright and adequate?		Add task lighting as needed. Bright lights should be located in ceiling above table, countertops, sinks, stove, and in pantry.
Smoke/Carbon Monoxide Detectors Are carbon monoxide and smoke detectors installed?		Install detectors in kitchen. Replace batteries semiannually.
Fire Extinguisher Is there a fire extinguisher in the kitchen?		Make sure fire extinguisher is usable and accessible.
Appliances and their Cords Are there appliances in the kitchen that your loved one cannot or should not use? Are there appliance cords that pose a danger?		Remove appliances that should not or cannot be operated by your loved one on their own. Make sure cords are not near sink or stove.
Counter Clutter Are kitchen counters cluttered?		Keep kitchen counters free of clutter that might cause confusion.
Kitchen Floor Is floor free of tripping hazards?		Remove all rugs, pet food bowls, cords, plants, or any other potential tripping hazards.
Labels Are things visibly and legibly labeled?		Create large-print labels for all switches and containers.

Home Safety Checklist: Kitchen		
Issue	**Y/N**	**Options**
Cabinets		
Are doorknobs and cabinet handles easy to use?		Label all cabinets and drawers, and replace difficult-to-use handles, pulls, or knobs.
Are the most-used items within easy reach?		Rearrange cabinets if needed to make the most-used items easiest to reach. Get long-handled grabbers if needed.
Is assistance required to open jars and cans?		Find adaptive tools that work best for your loved one.
Stove		
Does it work properly?		Make sure oven door and burner controls are easy to use and work properly.
Is it easy to use?		Label burners and knobs/controls. Clear all items on counters near stove.
Should it be used?		If your loved one has a cognitive issue and shows signs of improper stove use, the caregiver must decide to unplug/disconnect the stove. Improper use can be things like: placing items on top of burners forgetting something is cooking forgetting that stove or oven is hot
Microwave Oven		
Does your loved one know what it is and how to use it?		Remove or unplug unit if needed.

Home Safety Checklist: Kitchen		
Issue	**Y/N**	**Options**
Medication Are medications kept in the kitchen?		Designate a cabinet for your loved one's medication. If more than one person in home takes medication, use separate cabinets.
Step Stools Should a step stool be used?		Step stools can be a hazard and must not be used to reach items that are too high. Find an alternative to a stool if items cannot be stored within person's reach.
Refrigerator Is the food inside still good?		Designate someone to throw out old or rotten food. The person you are caring for may not know the difference.
Is the food inside covered and stored properly?		All food in refrigerator and freezer should be tightly covered and stored properly with a label including what it is and date it was stored. Do not store food on top of refrigerator –out of sight, out of mind!
Is a list of emergency contacts readily available on door?		Make sure emergency contact list and information is readily available in "File of Life" pouch on refrigerator door.

Home Safety Checklist: Living Area		
Issue	**Y/N**	**Options**
Lighting		
Is lighting adequate?		Room should be evenly lit throughout. Use task lighting and touch lamps as needed.
Flooring and Rugs		
Is the flooring free of clutter and tripping hazards?		Remove and replace loose floorboards. Area rugs are tripping hazards and should be removed. If floor is carpeted, make sure it has been stretched properly, and ensure there are no lumps or ridges.
Obstacles		
What are the obstacles in the room?		Remove ALL clutter. Organize and box for proper storage, donation, or disposal—no matter what the item is.
Is there excess furniture?		Remove unnecessary furniture.
Is there room to navigate?		Allow 5½ feet in between each piece of furniture to accommodate use of a wheelchair.
Are there doors in the room?		Keep all doors closed at all times.
Tables		
Are there glass-topped tables?		Remove all furniture with glass tops.

Home Safety Checklist: Living Area		
Issue	**Y/N**	**Options**
Tables and Shelving Are tables and shelves full of clutter?		Remove excess clutter from tables and shelves. Organize and box items for proper storage, disposal, or donation.
Chairs and Seating Is the seating comfortable and easy to use?		Use chairs with straight backs, armrests, and firm seats. Make sure seating is a sensible height. Sensible height is if person's thighs are parallel to floor and feet are flat on the floor when seated on the edge of the chair. If needed and possible, add firm cushion to existing pieces to add height. This will make it easier for your loved one to sit down and get up.
Mirrors Does mirror cause fear or confusion?		Mirrors may need to be covered or removed for those with dementia as the person may no longer recognize themselves. Mirrors can be removed or covered with a window shade that can be raised or lowered.
Cords Do they pose a tripping hazard?		Use extension cords sparingly. Secure to baseboards to move them out of the way and prevent tripping.

Home Safety Checklist: Laundry		
Issue	**Y/N**	**Options**
Lighting Is lighting adequate?		Room should be bright. Add lighting as needed.
Clutter and Organization Is room free of tripping hazards?		If possible, find a place—other than on the floor—to store laundry basket. Remove all unnecessary items and box for proper storage, donation, or disposal.
Supplies Are laundry supplies organized and properly labeled?		Organize and label laundry supplies.
Can laundry supplies be easily reached without stretching?		Ensure laundry supplies are within easy reach.
Washer and Dryer Are washer and dryer easy and convenient to use?		Washer and dryer should be located side by side so that wet clothes do not have to be moved from room to room.
Are dryer lint trap and vent hose cleaned regularly?		To prevent fires, clean lint trap and vent hose regularly.
Ventilation Is the room well ventilated?		Keep windows and/or doors open when in room for proper ventilation.

Home Safety Checklist: Basement		
Issue	**Y/N**	**Options**
Stairs		
Are there handrails on both sides of the steps?		Install railings as needed.
Do railings or steps have loose or uneven wood or potential for splinters?		Repair or replace wood that is loose or splintered.
Are items stacked on the steps?		Remove unnecessary items and box for storage, donation, or disposal.
Lighting		
Is lighting adequate?		Basement should be bright. Add lighting as needed.
Are light switches located at top and bottom of stairs?		Install additional switches as needed.
Clutter and Organization		
Is room free of trip hazards?		Remove unnecessary items and box for storage, donation, or disposal. If possible, find a place—other than on the floor—to store laundry basket.
Shelving		
Is shelving sturdy enough to hold items placed on it?		Remove unnecessary items and box for storage, donation, or disposal.
Are items on shelves neatly stacked so they will not fall off?		Shelving should be located at a height that person using it can reach items without stretching.
Frequently Used Items		
Are frequently used items within easy reach?		Organize items so that most-used items are easiest to reach.

Home Safety Checklist: Garage		
Issue	**Y/N**	**Options**
Stairs		
Are there handrails on both sides of the steps?		Install railings as needed.
Do railings or steps have loose or uneven wood or potential for splinters?		Repair or replace wood that is loose, uneven, or splintered.
Are items stacked on the steps?		Remove unnecessary items and box for storage, donation, or disposal.
Lighting		
Is lighting adequate?		Garage should be bright. Add lighting as needed.
Are light switches located at top and bottom of stairs?		Install additional switches as needed.
Tools and Equipment		
Are sharp tools away from walkways and hung or stored properly?		Hang or store sharp tools properly for safety and to prevent tripping hazards.
Is machinery or equipment blocking walkway?		Remove unnecessary items, and box for storage, donation, or disposal.
Are frequently used tools and equipment easily accessible?		Organize space so that most-used items are easily accessible.
Clutter and Organization		
Is room free of tripping hazards?		Remove unnecessary items and box for storage, donation, or disposal.

Home Safety Checklist: Garage		
Issue	**Y/N**	**Options**
Frequently Used Items Are frequently used items easily accessible?		If items are used inside the home, consider storing those items inside. Remove unnecessary items, and box for storage, donation, or disposal.
Garage Door Does garage door have an automatic opener?		Automatic garage door openers make it easier to get in and out of the garage. Check batteries in opener and in the main box semiannually.

Home Safety Checklist: Foyer		
Issue	**Y/N**	**Options**
Lighting Is lighting sufficient inside foyer and outside on porch?		Add lighting as needed.
Doorbell Can doorbell be heard all throughout home?		Repair or replace doorbell so that it can be heard anywhere in the home.
Door, Window, and Peephole Can you see who is standing on the front porch or stoop?		Clear window or install peephole to be able to identify people before opening the door.
Closet Is coat closet easy to use and not too cluttered? Is there room to store hats, scarves, gloves, and boots?		Remove unnecessary items and box for storage, donation, or disposal. If there is no closet, install sturdy hooks for coats, hats, scarves, and gloves.
Doormat Is there a doormat and is it appropriate?		Use an absorbent mat with a non-skid backing. Don't use a dark mat – a darker mat could be mistaken for a hole in the floor.
Door Can door be easily locked? Is there a dead bolt lock on the door?		If a person is in early stages of dementia, doors should be secured to prevent wandering. Install latches high on door so they cannot be easily reached.

Home Safety Checklist: Porch, Yard, Driveway		
Issue	**Y/N**	**Options**
Lighting Do exterior porch and garage lights illuminate entire areas? Is yard lighting equipped with motion detectors?		Add lighting or replace bulbs with the highest wattage the fixture allows. If possible, install motion detector lights for safety and security.
Steps and Rails Are there sturdy rails to use for climbing up and down stairs? Are rails smooth and free of splinters? Are there any loose or wobbly steps? Are steps slippery in wet conditions?		Repair or replace rails as needed to ensure proper sturdiness and safety. Repair or replace rails to prevent injury from cracks or splinters. Repair or replace any loose or wobbly steps to prevent trip/fall hazard. Add non-slip material to stair treads to prevent them from becoming slippery when wet.
Sidewalks and Driveway Do sidewalks and driveway have cracks or loose cement that could be trip hazards?		Repair any cracks or loose cement that could be potential trip hazards. Be aware of tree roots that may affect paved surfaces.
Mailbox Is there a clear path to the mailbox?		Make arrangements with the Post Office to have mail delivered to door for a person who is elderly or disabled.

Lighting, Glare, and Color Contrast

Depending on your loved one's vision, the severity of a brain injury or cognitive deficit, or individual preferences, you may find it necessary to modify existing lighting, glare, and contrast in the home. People will not always admit that they have an issue with their vision, but if they do, it will affect their ability to engage in an activity. Here are some tips to help:

Lighting

The following lighting changes could be key in your loved one's safety and ability to perform tasks independently.

- Fluorescent lighting can contribute to an increase in glare. Try different types of lightbulbs to see which is most comfortable for your loved one.
- Keep all rooms evenly lit and the lighting level consistent throughout

the home, so shadows and dangerous bright spots are eliminated.

- Make sure light switches, pull cords, and lamps are easily accessible for your loved one, particularly if he or she is in a wheelchair.
- If possible, purchase touch lamps or those that can be turned on or off by sound.
- Be certain that all stairwells are well lit and have handrails.
- Depending on the individual, additional task lighting may be necessary in certain areas of the home.
- Additional lighting for closets and smaller areas may be helpful. Battery-operated push lights are a good option.

Glare

Glare can be caused by sunlight or light from a lamp. When the light hits a shiny surface, such

as a magazine page or even a wall painted with high-gloss paint, the resulting glare can make it difficult for someone with low vision to see.

Sunglasses can be beneficial for someone who is light sensitive. Offer your loved one the opportunity to try different lens colors to see which works best.

- Sunlight can fill the room with light without producing glare. Adjust sunlight coming through windows by using mini blinds and altering their position throughout the day. If mini blinds are not available, use sheer curtains to diffuse the light.

- Be aware when placing mirrors in a room. Mirrors placed across from larger windows can significantly increase the amount of light in a room. This could be beneficial for someone who prefers the additional light.

- Cover bare lightbulbs with shades.

- Position chairs and tables so that when your loved one is sitting on a chair or at a table, they are not looking directly at the light coming from a window.

- Cover or remove shiny/reflective surfaces, such as floors and tabletops.

Color Contrasts

Using contrast is a good strategy if your loved one has a visual impairment. The more contrast, the easier it is to find and use objects or activity items around the house.

- Put light-colored objects against a dark background.

- Avoid upholstery with patterns for seated activities. Stripes, plaids, and checks can be visually confusing.

- Opt for solid-colored tables and countertops in a neutral tone.

Countertops with busy patterns can make it difficult to locate items and can be more difficult to keep clean.

- In a room with mostly dark tones, place light-colored pillows or chairs in strategic places to help your loved one find things and get around easily.

- If your loved one must, or is capable of maneuvering stairs, put contrasting stripes on the edges of each stair to make each stair visible and to prevent the stairs from disappearing from view.

Personal History Form

This is ____________________'s Personal History

***Note:** This form includes some questions that would be asked if your loved one has dementia symptoms.*

Name: ____

Maiden Name: __________________________________

Preferred Name: ________________________________

Date of Birth: __________________________________

Place of Birth: _________________________________

Name and relationship of people completing this Personal History Form: __________________________________

____

____

Diagnosis: ______________________________________

____

Describe the person's personality prior to the onset of the impairment. _________________________________

____

____

____

____

What makes the person feel valued? Talents, occupation, accomplishments, family, etc. ______________________

____

____

____

What are the daily living aids that must always be handy?

____

____

____

What are some favorite items they must always have in sight or close by? ____________________________

____

____

What is their exact morning routine? ________________

____

____

____

What is their exact evening routine? ________________

____

____

____

What type of clothing do they prefer? Do they like to choose their own clothes for the day, or do they prefer to have their clothes laid out by someone else?

____

____

____

____

____

What is their favorite beverage?

____

What is their favorite food?

____

____

What will get them motivated? (Church, friends coming over, going out, etc.)

____

____

____

____

____

____

____

____

List significant interests in their life, such as hobbies, recreational activities, job related skills/experiences, military experience, etc.

- Age 8 to 20:

  ____

  ____

  ____

- Age 20 to 40:

  ____

  ____

  ____

- Age 40+:

  ____

  ____

  ____

What is their religious background? (Affiliation, prayer time, symbols, traditions, church/synagogue name, etc. Did they lead any services or sing in the choir?)

____

____

____

____

What type of music do they enjoy listening to, playing, or singing? Do they have any musical talents?

____

____

____

What is their favorite TV program? Movie?

____

____

____

If reading has been a hobby, what authors, topics, or genres do they prefer? Would they listen to audiobooks or books on tape?

____

____

____

____

Marital status - If married more than once, provide specifics. Include names of spouses, dates of marriage, and other relevant information.

____

____

____

____

List distinct characteristics about their spouse(s), such as occupations, personality traits, or daily routine.

Do they have children? Be sure to include children both living and deceased. Include names, birth dates, and any other relevant information.

Do they have siblings? Be sure to include siblings both living and deceased. Include names, birth dates, and any other relevant information.

Who do they ask for the most? What is their relationship with this person(s)? Describe how that person typically spends their day.

____

____

____

____

What causes them stress? How is stress exhibited? Are there particular triggers like loud noises, white coats, or being ignored?

____

____

____

____

What calms them down when they are stressed or agitated?

____

____

____

____

How long has it been since symptoms first appeared?

____

____

Describe how the symptoms are affecting your loved one.

____

____

____

____

____

Have they accepted the changes in life since the diagnosis? ______________________________

____

____

What activities do they feel can no longer be participated in as a result of the impairment? And why?

____

____

____

____

What specific activities did they enjoy prior to the impairment?

____

____

____

____

Are they participating less frequently with family and friends? Can you identify why?

____

____

____

____

____

____

What age do you think the person thinks they are?

____

Do they ask for their spouse but do not recognize them?

____

Do they look for their children but do not recognize them?

____

Do they look for their mom? ______________________

Do they perceive themselves as younger? Please describe.

____

____

Describe the “home” they remember. ______________

____

____

____

Can they tell the difference between someone on TV and a real person?

Other information that would help to bring joy to your loved one.

P = past interest, **C** = currently engages in this activity, **NEW** = Has expressed interest in learning				
NAME:				
Interest	N/A	P	C	New
Arts and Crafts				
Knitting				
Sewing				
Crocheting				
Embroidering				
Scrapbooking				
Painting type:				
Coloring				
Woodworking				
Other				
Table Games				
Cards type:				
Bingo				
Dominoes				
Board Games				
Pokeno				
Jigsaw Puzzles				
Other:				
Spiritual				
Attend Church/Synagogue/Temple/Mosque				
Rosary Service				
Bible trivia				
Bible study				
Reading Bible/Torah/Koran/Watchtower				
Other:				

P = past interest, **C** = currently engages in this activity, **NEW** = Has expressed interest in learning				
NAME:				
Interest	N/A	P	C	New
Television / Movies				
Favorite channel:				
Movie types:				
Soap Operas:				
Game Shows:				
Talk Shows:				
Comedies:				
Dramas:				
News:				
Westerns:				
Cartoons:				
Adult Films:				
Other:				
Reading / Writing				
Book Club				
Type of Books:				
Large Print				
Talking Books				
Magazines:				
Legacy Kits/Autobiography				
Newspaper:				
Word Search				
Crossword Puzzles				
Letter Writing				
Other:				

P = past interest, **C** = currently engages in this activity, **NEW** = Has expressed interest in learning				
NAME:				
Interest	N/A	P	C	New
Sports Play or Watch				
Exercise:				
Baseball Team:				
Football Team:				
Soccer Team:				
Golf Player:				
Basketball Team:				
NASCAR Driver:				
Tennis Player:				
Other:				
Musical Interests				
Singing				
Listening to Radio/CD Type:				
Live Music				
Play Instrument:				
Movies / Videos				
Outdoor Activities				
Gardening				
Shopping / Outings				
Traveling				
Hunting				
Fishing				
Smoking				
Other:				

P = past interest, **C** = currently engages in this activity, **NEW** = Has expressed interest in learning				
NAME:				
Interest	N/A	P	C	New
Technology				
Computers / Internet				
Hand-held Video Games:				
TV Video Games:				
Other:				
Volunteering				
Distributing Mail:				
Newsletters:				
Church Groups:				
Service Projects:				
Other:				
Social Activities				
Men's Groups / Ladies' Groups / Young Person's Groups:				
Happy Hour				
Coffee Club				
Intergenerational Visits				
Discussion Groups				
History Groups				
Other				
Cooking:				
Animals:				
Political Interest:				
Manicures				
Other:				

About the Authors

Scott Silknitter

Scott Silknitter is the founder of R.O.S. Therapy Systems. He designed and created the R.O.S. Play Therapy™ System, the *How Much Do You Know About* Series of themed activity books and the R.O.S. *BIG Book*. Starting with a simple backyard project to help Mom and Dad, Mr. Silknitter has dedicated his life to improving the quality of life for all seniors through meaningful education, entertainment and activities.

Suzanne John, RN

Suzanne John is a retired Registered Nurse. She possesses over 12 years of clinical nursing experience in areas such as Cardiothoracic Surgical nursing, Medical and Cardiac Intensive Care nursing, working with ventilator-dependent patients and their families in a long-term care facility, Supervising RN in a skilled nursing facility, and as a RN providing outpatient cardiac rehab care to patients post open-heart surgery or after a "heart attack." Suzanne believes, "a nurse should be intelligent in her knowledge of the human body and medicine to practice safe care, but a nurse's success is obtained in her ability to interact and relate to her patient's condition and establish a trusting and respectful relationship." Suzanne currently teaches students studying to earn a caregiver certificate how to perform Activities of Daily Living.

Dawn Worsley, ADC/MC/EDU, CDP

Dawn Worsley is a Certified Activity Director with a specialization in Education and Memory Care, a Certified Eden Alternative Associate, and a Certified Dementia Practitioner. With over 20 years of experience, Ms. Worsley is an authorized certification instructor with the National Certification Council of Dementia Practitioners and a Modular Education Program for Activity Professionals course instructor.

References

1. *The Handbook of Theories on Aging* (Bengtson et al., 2009)
2. *Activity Keeps Me Going, Volume 1* (Peckham et al., 2011)
3. *Essentials for the Activity Professional in Long-Term Care* (Lanza, 1997)
4. *Abnormal Psychology*, Butcher
5. www.dhspecialservices.com
6. National Certification Council for Dementia Practitioners www.NCCDP.org
7. "Managing Difficult Dementia Behaviors: An A-B-C Approach" By Carrie Steckl
8. Iowa Geriatric Education Center website, Marianne Smith, PhD, ARNP, BC Assistant Professor University of Iowa College of Nursing
9. *Excerpts taken from "Behavior...Whose Problem is it?" Hommel, 2012
10. *Merriam-Webster's Dictionary*
11. "The Latent Kin Matrix" (Riley, 1983)
12. *Care Planning Cookbook* (Nolta et al.2007)
13. "Long-Term Care" (Blasko et al. 2011)
14. "Success Oriented Programs for the Dementia Client" (Worsley et al 2005)
15. Heerema, Esther. "Eight Reasons Why Meaningful Activities Are Important for People with Dementia." www.about.com
16. *Activities 101 for the Family Caregiver* (Appler-Worsley, Bradshaw, Silknitter)
17. American Foundation for the Blind
18. www.WebMD.com
19. www.nlm.nih.gov
20. www.caregiver.org
21. *Textbook of Medical-Surgical Nursing*, Brunner/Suddarth, 5th edition
22. http://www.nursing-theory.org/theories-and-models/roper-model-for-nursing-based-on-a-model-of-living.php

For additional assistance, please contact us at:
www.ROSTherapySystems.com
888-352-9788

Made in the USA
Charleston, SC
19 March 2016